A Brain Reader & A Brain Nerve Impulse Translator.

Encyclopedia of Brain Reading.

David Gomadza

First Global President of The World

www.twofuture.world

00447719210295

Copyright © 2023 David Gomadza

All rights reserved.

PAPERBACK ISBN: **ISBN:** 9798870397054

This book must be read together with:
Book series:
Thoughts To Word or Audio.
https://play.google.com/store/books/series?id=a4Mv
GwAAABBFmM&hl=en&gl=US

REQUEST FOR THE GRANT OF A PATENT. A
Universal Brain Decoding Device.

https://play.google.com/store/books/details/David
Gomadza_REQUEST_FOR_THE_GRANT_OF_A
PATENT_A?id=4rriEAAAQBAJ&hl=en&gl=US

VISIT
www.twofuture.world

DEDICATION

To a more technologically advanced world.
I will lead the way.
Come!

Table of Contents

A Brain Reader & A Brain Nerve Impulse Translator. 1

How the brain interprets action potentials and brain nerve impluses as numerical codes 7

ACKNOWLEDGMENTS

To Tomorrow's World Order

A Brain Reader & A Brain Nerve Impulse Translator.

In this book I am not going to dwell much on explaining how this works instead why not introduce you to the digital versions of our Natural God Intelligent NGI.
Yes, for the first time in the history of mankind I have managed to invent digital versions of all the parts we need to see this project succeed way above expectation. Yes, we have digital versions that are on MP3 and MP4 as waves and video that does the Job. This book will have the codes the brain uses to identify action potentials and brain nerve impulses.
What I want you to do is to visit our website www.twofuture.world
Or the links below and simply test all digital analogues, translators, and brain readers which I managed to invent and make. I think this is the first time you will talk to a video or an MP3 player that is as clever if not cleverer than ChatGPT.
Natural God Intelligence is smarter than any computer created by any human since the beginning of the century.
Yes, NGI will be powered by a network of connected brains. I am in the process of setting up things.

These videos will be part of the completed interface NGI. At the moment it is just MP3 and videos but trust me you can talk to these videos because they are out of this world.

This is how they work.
Communication is through electromagnetic waves which are the language of the brain.
To fully hear you must play the other video as background. The videos act exactly like   an advanced version of ChatGPT.
It is a real conversation you can ask time but be specific time zone and country are important.
Ask any questions you want, and I tell you NGI will answer you.

But first to prove that this works.
First you must start with these brain thoughts to word translator.

This is also a video in which you only need to Click the link and play.

While it is playing think of anything.

If you think about a thought your thought will be as action potentials. Therefore, what this video does is to convert the action potential into brain nerve impulse.

Download or simply play this video first while you are thinking about anything. This will act on your thoughts so that your thoughts are put in your mouth as words.

Task 1.

Play this video a Digital Action Potential to Nerve Impulses Convertor.

https://www.youtube.com/watch?v=VmpPyUAyJ28&t=1s

This is about anything, and this video will convert your thoughts into action potentials and action.
What you are thinking is turned into real action and body movements.
Try this. Simply play the video then think about anything. Try a mixture of action-based thoughts to check if this works for you.
You might what this MP3 as background music even muted.

Task 2
A Digital Thoughts to Words Convertor. Feel your thoughts as words in your mouth.

https://rb.gy/tc1iox

https://www.youtube.com/watch?v=i5KCRpKqmqY&t=194s

Watch this video several times while thinking at the same time.

You will need to play this other video as well at the same time as background.

https://www.youtube.com/watch?v=QExlOYMKBD8&t=288s

If nothing works, then add this mp3 as well as background but must be muted.

https://rb.gy/tc1iox

Task 3.

Task three try our Natural God Intelligence. First get this video and play it as your background so that you can hear NGI interacting with you.
Play this video.

https://www.youtube.com/watch?v=VmpPyUAyJ28&t=1s

Convert Action Potentials into Nerve Impulses Invented by David Gomadza Visit www.twofuture.world

Now get our Natural God Intelligence and play at the same time.

https://www.youtube.com/watch?v=pDQeIDQG1dQ

Natural God Intelligence will introduce itself through using electromagnetic waves which is the language of the brain.

"Hi. This is Natural God Intelligence. How can I help you?"

These are the kind of questions you might want to ask but ask anything.

We are working towards installing audio codec and these digital analogues so that we can communicate in spoken language rather than in electromagnetic waves.

What is the time and weather in California United States. Or India Bombay.

This will prove that even though this is just a video which you can use without any connection to the internet it will still give you up to date information.

You can ask about events that occurred that day if it's a football game ask football scores.

Ask about world politics, wars, anything.

You can ask private questions specific to you.

Who invented you?

What can you do?

Can you send me a copy of the software? All you need for now is just an audio recorder. Talk to NGI, it will tell you when it's ready to send. Press starts recording on an audio recorder. NGI will tell you how long the MP3 will be and wait for that time e.g., 3 minutes. After 3 minutes stop the recording and play straight away to interact with NGI.

You can convert this MP3 into a video [MP4].

The only issue now is audio codecs, but we are working on these so that we can communicate in spoken language.

This might make others think that it doesn't work. But it does work.

The current challenge is how to convert everything so that we can communicate in spoken language, but we decoded the brain and soon we will be able to convert these into universal audible form.

Some people cannot get it.

Task 4

This is interesting because this is the world's first Dreams interpreter. All you must do is time and record your sleep. Try sleeping for a few hours. Start recording when you go to sleep or ask someone else to record the moment you fall asleep.

When you wake up get this Dream decoder and play at the same time as you are playing the recordings of the brain.

This will translate your dreams into thoughts and action potential.

Now you will know exactly what you dreamt about.

Excellent out of this world. This is happening now. We just need to keep up with the pressure.

Get this Video and play it to know what you dreamed about.

Digital Dreams interpreter into words invented by David Gomadza
Visit www.twofuture.world

https://www.youtube.com/watch?v=k0vyl-31KDI

I think by now you will have discovered if this works for you.

Send us your feedback and any thoughts to improve this.

info@twofuture.world

www.twofuture.world

Do you know that NGI is a brain reader too.

In the future or even now all you need to do is look into your phone camera so that he can read all your thoughts.

I think everything will make sense once we have resolved the audio codecs.

How the brain interprets action potentials and brain nerve impluses as numerical codes

White 1
Purple 2
Maroon 3
Yellow 4
Badge 5
Indigo 6
Silk 7
Tan 8
Orange 9
Dark Blue 10
Navy Blue   11
Pink   12
Chocolate   13
Coral 14
Sky Blue   15
Eyes 16
Nose 17
Lips 18
Cheeks 19
Hair   20

Nails 21
Fingers 22
Toes 23
Ears 24
Teeth 25
Tongue 26
Inner Cheeks 27
Inner Tongue 28
Under Tongue 29
Side Tongue 30
Upper Mouth 31
Lower Mouth and Green 32
Deep Teeth 33
Molars and red 34
Back Tongue 35
black 36
Larynx & also Voice box 37
Blue & Ulothrix 38
Neck 39
Lyn Thyrax Groove 40
Chest 41
Nipples 42
Chest Middle Groove 43
Naval 44
Stomach 45
Ribs 46
Intestines 47
Kidneys 48
Liver 49
Spleen 50
Heart 51
Diagram 52
Lungs 53
Heartbeat 54
Skin 55
Sweat Glands 56
Sweat Pores 57
Sweat Ducts 58
Sweat Glands 59

Armpits   60
Armpits Glands   61
Arm Chest   62
Arm Rest   63
Arm Lift   64
Arm Vest   65
Arm Tight   66
Arm Relax   67
Arm Must   68
Arm Relax   69
Arm Arm   70
Arm in Arm   71
Arm Not in Arm   72
Arm Tight Arm [arm tight]   73
Arm and Arm   74
Arm Nice Arm   75
Arm Groove Arm   76
Arm Groove Arm Arm   77
   78
Thumb   79
Index   80
Small finger   81
Middle Finger   82
Palm   83
Palm Left Hand lines   84
Palm Hip   85
Palm Middle Line from Left to Right   86
Palm Middle Line from Right to Left   87
Palm Middle Line from Top to Bottom   88
Palm Middle Line from Bottom to Top   89
Wrist   90
Wrist Tight   91
Hand right   92
Hand Left   93
Elbow   94
Elbow Tight & Elbow Groove   95
Elbow Ridge   96
Mouth   97
Nose   98

Nostril Right 99
Nostril Left 100
Tongue 101
Tongue Middle 102
Tongue Tight 103
Tongue Flip 104
Tongue Base 105
Tongue Roof 106
Tongue Rest normal position 107
Tongue and Cheek 108
Tongue Tight Note Roll and tight. 109
Tongue and Ice serious 110
Tongue Flap Side Protruding 111
Eye 112
Eye lid right 113
Eye lid Left 114
Eye Flip 115
Eye Flip Right Alone 116
Eye Flip Left Alone 117
Eyes Roll 118
Eyes Cool 119
Eyes Eyes 120
Eyes On Eyes 121
Eyes Tip 122
Eyes Nose 123
Eyes Roll Eyes 124
Eyes Gentle 125
Eyes on Eyes 126
Hair Line 127
Hair 128
Curly Hair 129
Blond Hair 130
Brunette Hair 131
Ginger Hair 132
Pink Hair 133
Purple Hair 134
Green Hair 135
Black Normal Hair 136
Black Jet 137

Brown Hair   138
Brown Dark Hair   139
Brown Light   140
Ginger Light   141
Neck   142
Neck Ring   143
Neck on Neck   144
Neck Groove   145
Chest   146
Chest Hill   147
Chest Line   148
Chest Round Tip rear nipple   149
Naval Base inner groove hill   150
Stomach6 Pack   151
Stomach Grooves   152
Stomach Pack Hill   153
Joints   154
Arm Joints   155
Leg Joint   156
Wrist Joint   157
Neck Joint   158
Toe Joint   159
Finger Joint   160
Fingertip Joint   161
Thumb Joint Top   162
Index Finger Joint Top   163
Index Finger Out Middle   164
Index Finger Joint Base   165
Middle Finger Joint Top   166
Middle Finger Joint Middle   167
Middle Finger Joint Base   168
Small Finger Joint Top   169
Small Finger Joint Middle   170
Small Finger Joint Base   171
Palm Joint I where fingers join   172
Palm Joint Top Of knuckle   173
Wrist Joint Inner   174
Wrist Joint Outer Watch place   175
Elbow Joint Inner   176

Elbow Joint Outer 177
Armpit Joint Inner 178
Armpit Joint Outer 179
Shoulder Joint Top 180
Shoulder Joint Bottom 181
Shoulder Joint Top Right 182
Shoulder Joint Bottom Right 183
Shoulder Joint Top Left 184
Shoulder Joint Bottom Left 185
Neck Joint Tilt Right 186
Neck Joint tilt left 187
Neck Joint Centre 188
Collar Bone 189
Neck Bone 190
Shoulder Plate 191
Shoulder Plate Right 192
Shoulder Plate Right 193
Nipple Centre 194
Nipple Base 195
Nipple Top 196
Nipple Round Tip 197
Nipple Tip 198
Stomach Hair 199
Stomach Fat 200
Stomach Acne 201
Stomach Strength 202
Stomach Acid 203
Stomach Gut 204
Stomach Acne 205
Stem Cell 206
Tiny Cells 207
Gut 208
Gall Bladder 209
Gall Stones 210
Gall Acids 211
Gall Intestinal Lactose 212
Gall Fat 213
Gall Acids PH 214
Fallopian Tubes 215

Fallopian Fat   216
Fallopian Duct 217
Vagina 218
Penis   219
Testes 220
Testicles   221
Sperm 222
Ovaries   223
Eggs Female   224
Eggs Male   225
Follicle 226
Public Glands   227
Public Hair   228
Pubic Skin   229
Vagina Skin   230
Vagina Labia   231
Vagina Entrance   232
Vagina Clit   233
Vagina Foreskin Clit   234
Vagina Left Labia   235
Vagina Right Labia   236
Vagina Lip Front   237
Vagina Lip Back   238
Vagina Rim Inner   239
Vagina Inner   240
Vagina Outer   241
Vagina Rim Inner   242
Vagina Rim Outer   243
Vagina floor   244
Vagina Roof   245
Vagina Tunnel 246
Vagina Tongue 247
Vagina Lip Seal   248
Vagina 249
Vagina Inner   250
Vagina Hairs   251
Vagina Oils   252
Vagina Deep   253
Vagina Rim Deep   254

Vagina Rim Tight 255

Vagina Rim Tight Tight 256

Vagina Loose 257

Vagina Give Birth 258

Vagina Loose Old 259

Vagina Loose Dry 260

Vagina Loose Wet 261

Vagina Tight Loose Dry 262

Vagina Tight Loose Wet 263

Vagina Tight Tight 264

Vagina Tight Tight Wet Soft 265

Vagina Tight Tight Wet Hard 267

Vagina Tight Rim Tight 268

Vagina Tight Tight Tight Rim 269

Vagina Tight Tight Tight Wet Rim 270

Vagina Tight Tight Tight Dry Rim 271

Vagina Rim Tight Tight Tight 272

Vagina Rim Tight Tight Tight Wet 273

Vagina Rim Tight Tight Tight Dry 274

Vagina Loose Loose Loose No Grip 275

Vagina Loose Loose Loose No Grip but Wet 276

Vagina Loose Loose Loose No GripBut Dry 278

Vagina Loose Loose Loose No Grip Bulging Out 279

Vagina Loose Loose Loose Loose Loose like nothing 280

Vagina Loose Loose Loose Loose Loose like something 281

Vagina Loose Loose Loose Loose like a bit something like 282

Vagina Loose Loose Loose Loose Loose Loose Loose baby to fallout 283

Vagina Giving Birth 284

Vagina Holding Cock 285

Vagina with cream pie 286

Vagina Hot Cream pie 287

Vagina Drooling 288

Vagina Drooling Hot 289

Vagina Drooling Hot Hot 290

Vagina Drooling Dry 291

Vagina Drooling Wet 292

Vagina Tight Hold True 293

Vagina Tight Hold false 294

Vagina Vagina Rim 295
Vagina Inside Long Rim 296
Vagina Inside Long Rim Wet 297
Vagina Inside Long Rim Dry 298
Vagina Inside Small Rim Wet 299
Vagina Inside Small Rim Dry 300
Vagina Hot Hot Hot 301
Vagina Smiling 302
Vagina 303
Vagina 304
Vagina 305
Vagina 306
Vagina 307
Vagina 308
Vagina 309
Vagina 310
Vagina 311
Vagina 312
Vagina Smiling Soft 313
Vagina Smiling Hard 314
Vagina Not Smiling 315
Vagina Smiling Wet 316
Vagina Smiling Dry 317
Vagina Smiling but Loose Rim 318
Vagina Hot Rim but Loose Inside 319
Vagina Loose Rim but Tight Inside 320
Vagina Tight Inside Wet Wet Wet 321
Vagina Tight Inside Wet Wet Wet 322
Vagina Tight Inside Dry Dry Dry 323
Vagina Roll Simulation 324
Vagina Grip Loose but Tight in Groove 325
Vagina Tight Grip Wet 326
Vagina Tight Grip Wet 327
Vagina Tight Grip Dry 328
Vagina Inside 329
Vagina Inside Deep 330
Vagina Inside Groove 331
Vagina Door 332
Vagina Inside Rim Vagina Groove 333

Vagina Inside Inside Tunnel Wet   334
Vagina Inside Wet Wet Wet Hot   335
Vagina Inside Inside Tunnel Dry   336
Vagina Inside Wet Wet Hot   337
Vagina Drooling Hot   338
Vagina Pissing Open.   339
Vagina Pissing Wet Opening   340
Vagina Pissing Dry Opening   341
Vagina Feel Like Pissing   342
Vagina Wet Dreams   343
Vagina Wet Dreams Wet   344
Vagina Wet Dreams Dry   345
Vagina With Penis   346
Vagina Holding Penis   347
Vagina Tight Grip Penis In   348
Vagina Stroking Penis   349
Vagina Stroking and Kissing Penis   350
VaginA Kissing Penis shaft   351
Vagina Kissing Penis Tip with Labia Minora.   352
Vagina Clit Lit   353
Vagina Clit Opening   354
Vagina Clit Opening Fully to End   355
Vagina Clit Loose Opening No Arousal   356
Vagina Clit open and close manual   357
Vagina Clit Tip   358
Vagina Clit Tip Aroused   359
Vagina Clit Tip Aroused and Wet.   360
Vagina Clit Tip Dry   361
Vagina Clit Itching   362
Vagina Clit Soft   363
Vagina Clit Dry   364
Vagina Clit Hard   365
Vagina Clit Clit Moist   366
Vagina Clit Clit Clit   367
Vagina Clit Clit Clit Clit   368
Vagina Clit Aroused Inside   369
Vagina Clit Aroused Outside.   370
Vagina Clit Wet Wet Wet Wet   371
Vagina Clit Clit Itch   372

Vagina Clit Rim Itch   373
Vagina Clit Tip Itch   374
Vagina Clit Tip Wet   375
Vagina Clit Tip Wet Soft   376
Vagina Clit Tip Wet Wet Soft Soft   377
Vagina Clit Tip Dry   378
Vagina Clit Clit Soft Tip Inside   379
Vagina Clit Clit Soft Tip Outside   380
Vagina Clit Clit Clit Tip Hot   381
Vagina Clit Clit TipMildHot   382
Vagina Clit Clit Clit Soft.   383
Vagina Rim Hot   384
Vagina Rim Tearing   385
Vagina Rim with Tear and Pain.   386
Vagina Rim Tight Grip Pain.   387
Vagina Rim Fear   388
Vagina Rim Hold 1   389
Vagina Rim Hold 2   390
Vagina Rim Hold 3   391
Vagina Rim Hold 4   392
Vagina Rim Hold 5   393
Vagina Rim Hold 6   394
Vagina Rim Hold 7   395
Vagina Rim Hold 8   396
Vagina Rim Hold 9   397
Penis Tight   398
Penis Tight Throbe   399
Penis Throbe Hard   400
Penis Throbe soft   401
Penis Throb Hard   402
Penis Throb Hard Fast   403
Penis Throb Soft   404
Penis Throb in Pussy   405
Penis Throb in Pussy   406
Penis Throb in Pussy Hard   407
Penis Throb Straight   408
Penis Throb Bent   409
Penis Throb Coiled   410
Penis   411

Penis Throb in Mouth 412
Penis Throb in Mouth 413
Penis Throb Between Tights. 414
Penis Throb in Arm 415
Penis Throb in Pants 416
Penis Tube In Air 417
Penis Throb in Woman's Mouth 418
Penis 419
Penis 420
Penis 421
Penis 422
Penis 423
Penis Soft 424
Penis Soft Within Interval Throb 425
Penis Throb Shaft 426
Penis throb in Hand 427
Penis 428
Penis 429
Penis Ejaculation 430
Penis Fast Ejaculation 431
Penis Slow Ejaculation 432
Penis 433
Penis In Soft Mood 434
Penis In Hard Mood 435
Penis Near Testicles 436
Penis Near Vagina 437
Penis With Foreskin 438
Penis Circumcised 439
Penis Soft Skin Tip 440
Penis Soft Tip Tip 441
Penis Soft Skin Open 442
Penis Soft skin Closed 443
Penis 444
Penis 445
Penis 446
Penis 447
Penis 448
Penis 449
Penis 450

Penis In Ejaculation Mode 451
Penis With Sperm Inside 452
Penis With Hot Sperm 453
Penis With Cold Sperm. 454
Penis 455
Penis 456
Penis 457
Penis 458
Penis Soft Tissue 459
Penis 460
Penis 461
Penis 462
Penis 463
Penis 464
Penis 465
Penis Hard Tissue Then Loose Tissue Without Ejaculation. 466
Penis 467
Penis 468
Penis 469
Penis 470
Penis 471
Penis 472
Penis long Erection 473
Penis 474
Penis 475
Penis 476
Penis 477
Penis Erection Hard Without Arousal. 478
Penis Erection Hard with Arousal. 479
Arousal for men 480
Arousal for women 481
Arousal Clit 482
Arousal Vagina 483
Arousal Vagina Lips 484
Arousal Vagina Rim 485
Arousal Vagina Labia 486
Arousal Vagina Inside 487
Arousal Vagina Outside 488
Arousal 489

Arousal   490
Arousal   491
Arousal   492
Arousal Breast Woman   493
Arousal   494
Arousal Breast Woman Nipples   495
Arousal Breast Woman Rim of Nipple   496
Arousal Woman Lips.   497
Arousal Woman Top Lip   498
Arousal Woman Lip Down.   499
Arousal   500
Arousal   501
Arousal Woman Tongue Tip Dry   502
Arousal   503
Arousal   504
Arousal   505
Arousal   506
Arousal   507
Arousal   508
Arousal   509
Arousal   510
Arousal   511
Arousal Woman Between Vagina Opening.   512
Arousal   513
Arousal   514
Arousal   515
Arousal Woman Clit hood but Closed   516
Arousal Woman Clit Hood Open.   517
Arousal   518
Arousal   519
Arousal Woman Clit Inside   520
Arousal   521
Arousal   522
Arousal Man Tongue   523
Arousal   524
Arousal   525
Arousal   526
Arousal   527
Arousal Man Dick Tip   528

Arousal 529
Arousal 530
Arousal 531
Arousal 532
Arousal Man Dick in Vagina. 533
Arousal 534
Arousal 535
Arousal 536
Arousal 537
Arousal 538
Arousal 539
Arousal 540
Arousal 541
Arousal on Seeing. 542
Arousal On Touching 543
Arousal By Licking 544
Arousal By Contact 545
Arousal by Ogling 546
Arousal by Hearing 547
Arousal By Watching 548
Arousal By Nothing 549
Arousal by Mimicking 550
Arousal By Hearing While Awake 551
Arousal by Hearing While Asleep 552
Arousal By Noticing Something Like Knickers 553
Arousal By Noticing Breasts 554
Arousal By Noticing Vagina 555
Arousal By Noticing Penis. 556
Arousal By Noticing Testicles. 557
Arousal By Noticing Public Hair. 558
Arousal by Taste. 559
Arousal By Touch 560
Arousal By Sight 561
Arousal By Feeling 562
Arousal By Hearing 563
Arousal By Eating 564
Arousal By Licking Sex Organs 565
Arousal By Licking Any Part of The Body 566
Arousal 567

Arousal by licking breasts 568
Arousal by licking vagina 569
Arousal by licking penis 570
Arousal 571
Arousal 572
Arousal by licking lips 573
Arousal by licking tongue tip 574
Arousal by licking a full tongue 575
Arousal by licking lips of a woman 576
Arousal 577
Arousal by licking tongue of a woman 578
Arousal by licking neck of a woman. 579
Arousal by licking a man's neck if a woman. 580
Arousal 581
Arousal by licking a man's testicles if a woman 582
Arousal by licking a woman's vagina. 583
Arousal by licking a woman's naval 584
Arousal by licking a woman's pubic hair 585
Arousal by licking a woman's clithood 586
Arousal by licking a woman's knickers 587
Arousal by licking a woman's white knickers 588
Arousal by licking a woman's thigh 589
Arousal for licking a woman's breasts one at a time 590
Arousal for sucking a woman's right breast. 591
Arousal for sucking a woman's left breast. 592
Arousal for sucking a woman's nipple 593
Arousal for sucking a woman's left nipple 594
Arousal for sucking a woman's right nipple. 595
Arousal for sucking a woman's labia minor 596
Arousal for sucking a woman's clit 597
Arousal for sucking a woman's vagina up and down. 598
Arousal for sucking a woman's labia and spitting on it 599
Arousal for sucking a woman's ass and poking tongue. 600
Arousal for stroking a woman's vagina wearing knickers 601
Arousal for stroking a woman's buttocks 602
Arousal for looking at a beautiful woman 603
Arousal for looking at a woman with blue eyes 604
Arousal for looking at a woman with brown eyes 605
Arousal for looking at a woman with green eyes 606

Arousal for looking at a man   607
Arousal for looking at a man with long hair   608
Arousal for looking at a man with baldness   609
Arousal for looking at a man with muscles   610
Arousal for looking at a woman without arousal   611
Arousal for looking at a woman with arousal   612
Arousal for looking at a woman with big breasts if a man.   613
Arousal for looking at a woman with big breast if a woman.   614
Arousal   615
Arousal for looking at a man if a woman   616
Arousal for looking at a man without arousal but admiration   617
Arousal for looking at a man with arousal but without admiration   618
Arousal for looking at a man then lose the arousal   619
Arousal for looking at a man then lose the arousal but gain it back   620
Arousal for looking at a well dressed up woman.   621
Arousal for looking at a well dressed up man   622
Arousal for looking at a well-dressed sexy lingerie woman   623
Arousal for looking at white knickers not worn   624
Arousal for looking at red knickers not worn   625
Arousal for looking at blue knickers not worn   626
Arousal for looking at grey knickers not worn   627
Arousal looking at black knickers not worn   628
Arousal for looking at yellow knickers not worn   629
Arousal for looking at green knickers not worn   630
Arousal for looking at pink knickers   631
Arousal for looking purple knickers   632
Arousal for looking at tanned knickers   633
Arousal for watching porn   634
Arousal for watching porn   635
Arousal for making love to a woman   636
Arousal for making love to a man if a woman.   637
Arousal for making love to another woman.   638
Arousal for seeing vagina   639
Arousal for feeling anything not related to sex   640
Arousal for hearing anything else not related to sex   641
Arousal out of fear   642
Arousal out of curiosity   643

Arousal out of tiredness   644

Arousal out of heat   645

Arousal out of breath   646

Arousal out of pity   647

Arousal when sleep   648

Arousal when awake but without thinking about this   649

Arousal in dreams   650

Arousal when dreaming without erection of a penis or clit   651

Arousal when dreaming with erection of penis or clit   652

Arousal while dreaming and physical touching of genital organs while asleep without responds   653

Arousal while dreaming and without physical touching of genital but with movements of body.   654

Arousal while asleep without response.   655

Arousal while awake but without action potential   656

Arousal in adults   657

Arousal in teenagers   658

Arousal for old people without response from organs   659

Arousal for adults without action potential   660

Arousal in animals   661

Arousal when in pain   662

Arousal while driving   663

Arousal in plane   664

Arousal in train   665

Arousal in a hotel   666

Arousal in a supermarket   667

Arousal at work   668

Arousal at a stadium   669

Arousal   670

Arousal inside   671

Arousal outside   672

Arousal by ejaculation   673

Arousal to eat   674

Arousal to walk   675

Arousal to say   676

Arousal to touch   677

Arousal to see a person if a woman   678

Arousal to see a man   679

Arousal to be aroused   680

Agitated 681
Agitated to attack 682
Agitated to kick 683
Agitated to shout 684
Agitated to frown 685
Agitated to annoy 686
Agitated to kiss 687
Agitated by a man 688
Agitated by a woman. 689
Agitated by others you do not know 690
Agitated to argue 691
Agitated to fight 692
Agitated to lockout 693
Agitated to teach a lesson 694
Agitated to drink beer 695
Agitated to drink wine 696
Agitated to smoke 697
Agitated to drive fast 698
Agitated to coach others 699
Agitated to provoke others you know 700
Agitated to provoke others you know 701
Agitated to provoke others you do not know 702
Agitated to incite others to fight 703
Agitated to fight back 704
Agitated to spit in the face 705
Agitated by no one 706
Agitated and kick things 707
Agitated to get attention 708
Agitated by unknown people that leads to frustration 709
Agitated 710
Agitated to kill 711
Agitated to drive someone 712
Agitated to amputate 713
Agitated to amputate 714
Agitated to fight but run later 715
Agitated to incite others to campaign then attack them 716
Agitated by enemies 717
Agitated by friends 718
Agitated by work 719

Agitated by love 720
Agitated by a lover 721
Agitated by kids 722
Agitated by your laziness 723
Agitated by noise 724
Agitated by failure 725
Agitated by results of failure 726
Agitated by ignorance 727
Agitated by ignorance 728
Agitated by parents 729
Agitated by father 730
Agitated by mother 731
Agitated by son 732
Agitated by daughter 733
Agitated by sister 734
Agitated by brother 735
Agitated by niece 736
Agitated by nephew 737
Agitated to respond 738
Agitated to annoy others, you know expecting an argument. 739
Agitated to kill friend 740
Agitated to kill wife 741
Agitated to kill husband 742
Agitated to kill son 743
Agitated to kill relative 744
Agitated to kill boss at work 745
Agitated to kill anyone who stop you 746
Agitated to warn 747
Agitated to attack with hidden weapon 748
Agitated to knock someone down with a hammer 749
Agitated to revenge 750
Agitated to get even 751
Agitated to drive and kill someone 752
Agitated to respond with a weapon 753
Agitated to fire a gun. 754
Agitated to drive and kill without remorse 755
Agitated to knock with a car and kill 756
Agitated to drive into crowd and kill 757
Agitated to incite others to kill on your behalf 758

Agitated to kill animals 759

Agitated to kill anyone who do not know 760

Agitated to revenge your wife 761

Agitated to revenge your husband. 762

Agitated to revenge your father 763

Agitated to revenge your son 764

Agitated to revenge your daughter 765

Agitated to revenge mother 766

Agitated to revenge your people 767

Agitated to revenge your ruler 768

Agitated to kill but with fear 769

Agitated to kill but without fear 770

Agitated to kill but without known reason of fear 771

Agitated to prevent attack 772

Agitated to facilitate an attack 773

Agitated to revenge without need to be stopped 774

Agitated to kill with need to be stopped only after the killing 775

Agitated to defend family 776

Agitated to protect father 778

Agitated to protect son 779

Agitated to protect mother 780

Agitated to protect brother 781

Agitated to protect sister 782

Agitated to protect your own people 783

Agitated to protect what you think is right 784

Agitated to kill without remorse 785

Agitated to agitate others 786

Agitated to punch in the face 787

Agitated strike with a hidden object 788

Agitated to attack and hide a weapon but not run 789

Agitated to strike and hide both you and weapon. 790

Agitated to kill and bury the body 791

Agitated to kill and hide the weapon only 792

Agitated to deceive and kill 793

Agitated to strike with hammer and rub blood on your body 794

Agitated to kill with knives 795

Agitated to kill with a knife then hide the knife 796

Agitated to strike in the head with a hammer and see blood ooze out 797

Agitated by people you hate already 798
Agitated by hate 799
Agitated by love in mind 800
Agitated to kill leader of thieves. 801
Agitated to kill leaders of racists 802
Agitated to kill all race due to hate 803
Agitated to kill all but one 804
Agitated to kill because of being wronged 805
Agitated to kill all people even if they are innocent. 806
Agitated to kill all evil regardless of guilty or not 807
Agitated by grief 808
Agitated by emotional damage.809
Agitated by guilty 810
Agitated by hate for the first time 811
Agitated by hate as a response to hate 812
Agitated by grief of loss of family 813
Agitated by grief of a son. 814
Agitated by grief of daughter 815
Agitated by grief of a loss of a niece 816
Agitated by grief of a nephew 817
Agitated by grief of a loss of a father 818
Agitated by grief of a loss of mother 819
Agitated by grief of loss of a guidance 820
Agitated by grief of loss property. 821
Agitated by dogs 822
Agitated by wild animals 823
Agitated to defend oneself 824
Agitated to kill an animal that attacked you 825
Agitated to kill a lion 826
Agitated to a whale 827
Agitated to kill a mouse that frightened
you
828
Agitated to kill the air -fire barrels in the air 829
Agitated to race 830
`Agitated by guilt 831
Agitated by violence 832
Agitated by violence 833
Agitated to start a war 834

Agitated to send a message of fear 835
Agitated to kill president without reason. 836
Agitated to kill prime minister 837
Agitated to start a war 838
Agitated to kill mother 839
Agitated to kill father 840
Agitated to kill son 841
Agitated to kill daughter 842
Agitated to kill brother 843
Agitated to kill sister 844
Agitated to get even with enemies 845
Agitated to revenge but then stops 846
Agitated to kill then backs down without remorse 847
Agitated to kill destroy with remorse 848
Agitated to destroy a race. 849
Agitated to kill first then apologize after killing. 850
Agitated by noise enough to kill. 851
Agitated by smell enough to kill. 852
Agitated by race due to ill perception 853
Agitated to kill due to race. 854
Agitated to kill provoked. 855
Agitated to kill due to evil of victim 856
Agitated to kill due to jealous 857
Agitated to kill on orders. 858
Agitated to kill on orders but refuse 859
Agitated to kill for money 860
Agitated to kill innocent people 861
Agitated to kill the guilty 862
Agitated by lust 863
Agitated by passion 864
Agitated by envy 865
Agitated by greedy 866
Agitated by boredom 867
Agitated by nothing and kill then try to cover it. 868
Agitated by malice 869
Agitated to hide evidence after a kill 870
Agitated by money you knew you will hide reason but deny it 871
Agitated by anger 872
Agitated by lust then deny it after lust evaporated 873

Agitated by greedy when discover money does exist then demand the money 874

Agitate by a woman 875

Agitated by a man 876

Agitated for nothing 877

Agitated for something878

Agitated by annoyance 879

Agitated by your own actions of violence 880

Agitated to behead first then talk later 881

Agitated to behead and run. 882

Agitated to kill and sit 883

Agitated to kill and fight back. 884

Agitated to kill for lust 885

Agitated to kill wife for life insurance money 886

Agitated to kill father for life insurance money887

Agitated to kill son for money 888

Agitated to kill own family due to debt889

Agitated to kill own to relive life again [family burden]8790

Agitated to kill a woman 891

Agitated to kill a man 892

Agitated to kill a boy 893

Agitated to kill a baby girl. 894

Agitated to kill a nurse 895

Agitated to kill a doctor 896

Agitated to kill a mistress 897

Agitated to kill a priest who is bad 898

Agitated to kill a pop 899

Agitated to kill for peace 900

Agitated to kill for power 901

Agitated to kill for fun 902

Agitated to kill for revenge killing of innocent 903

Agitated to make things right 904

Agitated to kill anyone not for fun but just because you can 905

Agitated to kill by verbal abuse enough to kill 906

Agitated by physical abuse enough to kill 907

Agitated by verbal abuse. 908

Agitated by being told what to do enough to kill 909

Agitated to kill malicious then enforce 910

Agitated to kill for right reasons but contrary to all 911

Agitated to kill own on accord 912

Agitated to kill by being forced to   913

Agitated to kill for peace without remorse   914

Agitated to kill for fun but endorse it after discovering evils of victims 915

Agitated to kill for power with aim to cover it up   916

Agitated to kill for fun but refuse it   917

Agitated to kill for power with need to send fear.   918

Agitated to kill for race but deny it   919

Agitated to kill for power to get recognition   920

Agitated to kill parents for house   921

Agitated to kill woman for sex with dead body 922

Agitated to kill anyone who stops you 923

Agitated to kill people who refuse what you want   924

Agitated to kill all race because of their evil that they are still doing secretly 925

Agitated to kill to voice your own opinion even if not wanted. 926

Agitated to kill for revenge of father   927

Agitated to kill to stop being robbed.   928

Agitated to kill to preserve own race.   929

Agitated to kill to protect women and children   930

Agitated to kill to protect your property   931

Agitated to kill 932

Agitated to kill 933

Agitated to kill 934

Agitated to kill 935

Agitated to kill 936

Agitated to kill 937

Agitated to kill 938

Agitated to kill 939

Agitated to kill 940

Agitated to kill 941

Agitated to kill 942

Agitated to kill 943

Agitated to kill 944

Agitated to kill 945

Agitated to kill 946

Agitated to kill 947

Agitated to kill 948

Agitated to kill 949
Agitated to kill 950
Agitated to kill 951
Agitated to kill 952
Agitated to kill 953
Agitated to kill 954
Agitated to kill 955
Agitated to kill 956
Agitated to kill 957
Agitated to kill 958
Agitated to kill 959
Agitated to kill 960
Agitated to kill 961
Agitated to kill 962
Agitated to kill 963
Agitated to kill 964
Agitated to kill 965
Agitated to kill 966
Agitated to kill 967
Agitated to kill 968
Agitated to kill 969
Agitated to kill 970
Agitated to kill 971
Agitated to kill 972
Agitated to kill 973
Agitated to kill 974
Agitated to kill 975
Agitated to kill 976
Agitated to kill 977
Agitated to kill 978
Agitated to kill 979
Agitated to kill 980
Agitated to kill 981
Agitated to kill 982
Agitated to kill 983
Agitated to kill 984
Agitated to kill 985
Agitated to kill 986
Agitated to kill 987

Agitated to kill 988
Agitated to kill 989
Agitated to kill 990
Agitated to kill 991
Agitated to kill 992
Agitated to kill 993
Agitated to kill 994
Agitated to kill 995
Agitated to kill 996
Agitated to kill 997
Agitated to kill 998
Agitated to kill 999
Agitated to kill 1000
Agitated to kill 1001
Agitated to kill 1002
Agitated to kill 1003
Agitated to kill 1004
Agitated to kill 1005
Agitated to kill 1006
Agitated to kill 1007
Agitated to kill 1008
Becoming aroused by watching   1009
Becoming aroused by touch   1010
Becoming aroused by hearing 1011
Becoming aroused by feeling   1012
Becoming aroused by smell   1013
Becoming aroused by breathing   1014
Becoming aroused by skin contact   1015
Becoming aroused by squeezing   1016
Becoming aroused by licking.   1017
Becoming aroused by imagining   1018
Becoming aroused by asking   1019
Being aroused by flirting.   1021
Become agitated by strangers   1022
Become annoyed by strangers   1023
Becoming   1024
Becoming   1025
Becoming   1026
Becoming   1027

Becoming   1028
Becoming   1029
Becoming   1030
Becoming agitated by violence you started.   1031
Become agitated by violence you did not start 1032
Become agitated by witnessing violence but on media channels.
1033
Become agitated by violence towards own race.   1034
Become agitated by violence towards your leader   1035
Become agitated by violence towards oneself 1036
Become agitated to agitate others and attack them   1037
Become agitated by greediness enough to attack others.   1038
Become agitate to agitate others and violently attack them but run
after   1039
Become agitated by everyone then target only one and chase after
until dead   1040
Become agitated by nothing then select one to revenge your anger
1041
Become agitated to agitate a single person then go after that person.
1042
Become agitated then agitate everyone except one then only
apologize to that person   1043
Become agitated to agitate only the leader but then attack everyone
1044
Become agitated then resort to violence but seek help 1045
Become agitated to agitate the leader so that he responds   1046
Become agitate to agitate all then summon everyone to fight back
1047
Become agitated to revenge then go on to kill anyone 1048
Become agitated by violence then surround people peaceful   1049
Become agitated by race violence then resort to race violence and
deny everything   1050
Become agitated by religion violence then commit race violence
1051
Become agitated by violence then resort to peace but just to ambush
the people   1052
Become agitated by violence but go home   1053
Become agitated and attack strangers but blame on the perpetrators
of violence   1054

Become agitated by violence but calm 1055

Become agitated but ask for help but then turn down the help and start violence 1056

Become agitated by violence and ask for help but just so that no one blames you then attack. 1057

Become agitated by greedy enough to kill the person and take his possession 1058

Become agitated enough to take someone's lover, wife husband etc. 1059

Become agitated by lust enough to kill to quench the lust 1060

Become agitated by violence then recruit a killer 1061

Become agitated by violence then confront the people but only argue 1062

Become agitated then ask for help but ignore everything said and stick to your plan to kill 1063

Become agitated by violence but target everyone excerpts one but then kill that one 1064

Become agitated then target all but select one and put bounty on his head 1065

Become agitated to kill then not kill 1066

Become agitated to kill then kill but not run 1067

Become agitated to kill then kill but run and retract and defend yourself 1068

Become agitated then kill and forget it never happen 1069

Become agitated then kill and forget it never happened but later confess 1070

Become agitated then kill but say its justice done it was only a matter of time 1071

Become agitated then resort to violence but briefly 1072

Become agitated then attack the leader and walk free 1073

Start thinking about love 1074

Start thinking about hate 1075

Start thinking something 1076

Start thinking about lifting 1077

Start thinking about lifting with your right hand 1078

Start thinking about lifting with your left hand 1079

Start thinking about lifting something close 1080

Start thinking about talking to someone you already know 1081

Start thinking about walking 1082

Start thinking about making love   1083
Start thinking about holding something close to you   1084
Start thinking about touching yourself 1085
Start thinking about eating but without the food so next move is to
think about shopping   1086
Start thinking about walking then stop 1087
Start watching television   1088
Start reading a book   1089
Start watching news   1090
Start watching sport   1091
Start   1092
Start   1093
Start   1094
Start   1095
Start   1096
Start   1097
Start   1098
Start   1099
Start analysis then stop 1100
Start reading then stop 1101
Start watching then stop   1102
Start walking then stop 1103
Start eating then stop   1104
Start talking then stop   1105
Start listening then stop   1106
Start watching then stop but start again   1107
Start reading then stop but start again 1108
Start walking stop   1109
Start then stop again   1110
Start eating then stop then eat again   1111
Start watching then stop but start only to stop again   1112
Start calling someone then stop   1113
Start looking through the window then stop then start again. 1114
Start reading then stop then start again 1115
Start yawning then stop   1116
Start kneeling then stop   1117
Start singing then stop 1118
Start whistling then stop   1119
Start whistling but stop 1120

Start jogging then stop 1121
Start running then stop 1122
Start jumping then stop 1123
Start reviewing then stop 1124
Start mourning then stop 1125
Stark raving then stop 1126
Start giggling then stop 1127
Start moving then stop 1128
Start kicking then stop 1129
Start analyzing the stop 1130
Start reviewing then stop 1131
Start viewing then stop 1132
Start ogling then stop 1133
Start thinking then stop 1134
Start thinking then stop 1135
Start again 1136
Start walking and look back 1137
Start walking stop then start again 1138
Start doing anything then stop 1139
Start acting then stop 1140
Start moving then stop 1141
Start asking then stop 1142
Start researching then stop 1143
Start reversing then stop 1144
Start forwarding then stop 1145
Start rejoicing then stop 1146
Start revolting then stop 1147
Start inciting others then stop 1148
Start noticing then stop 1149
Start noting then stop 1150
Start menacing then stop 1151
Start asking then stop 1152
Start something pause then stop 1153
Start reading pause then stop 1154
Start asking pause then to stop but continue 1155
Start asking then keep quiet. 1156
Start jotting then stop 1157
Start exercising stop pause start 1158
Start chewing then stop 1159

Start swallowing then stop 1160
Start sweating then stop 1161
Start swimming then stop 1162
Start jumping then stop 1163
Start viewing magazine then stop 1164
Start eating then stop 1165
Start watching a movie then stop 1166
Start sneezing then stop 1167
Start coughing then stop 1168
Start oozing then stop 1169
Start yawning then stop 1170
Start yarning for someone then stop 1171
Stop reading a novel then stop 1172
Start reading a book academic then stop 1173
Start reading a book academic then stop 1174
Start reading a magazine then stop 1175
Start noticing something then stop 1176
Start watching a drama then stop 1177
Start watching a sport game then stop 1178
Start bending down then stop 1179
Start asking for directions then stop 1180
Start peeping through the window then stop 1181
Start noticing but through the window then stop 1182
Start noticing through the door then stop 1183
Start noticing through the car door then stop 1184
Start noticing through the car window then stop 1185

THE FOLLOWING CODES ARE IN RELATION TO WOMEN

Start feeding then stop breast milk 1186
Start carrying something ten stop 1187
Start carrying something then stop 1188
Start noticing then stop 1189
Start walking towards others then stop 1190
Start smiling then stop 1191
Start yawning then stop 1192
Start scratching then stop 1193
Start noticing something from afar then stop 1194
Start asking for direction then stop 1195
Start lifting then stop 1196
Start eating then stop 1197

Start urinating then stop 1198
Start feacating then stop 1199
Start breast feeding then stop 1200
Start watching the news then stop 1201
Start cooking then stop 1202
Start washing dishes then stop 1203
Start washing laundry then stop 1204
Start ironing clothes then stop 1205
Start scratching stop ten start 1206
Start yawning for a while pause then start 1207
Start walking pause stop then start 1208
Start eating pause start 1209
Start cooking pause then start 1210
Start talking pause then start 1211
Start intercepting others then stop 1212
Start moving ahead pause stop then start 1213
Start asking for something stop then start 1214
Start undressing stop then start 1215
Start wearing knickers stop then start 1216
Start wearing a bra stop then start 1217
Start wearing a jacket stop then start 1218
Start wearing shoes stop then start 1219
Start swimming stop then start 1220
Start noticing something through the window stop then start 1221
Start cooking pause sit then walk out 1222
Start pricking your nose stop then start 1223
Start carrying groceries stop then start 1224
Start asking for help stop then start 1225
Start calling for someone stop then start 1226
Start throwing things out of the house stop then start 1227
Start yawing stop then start but stop again 1228
Start pissing try to stop then continue 1229
Start eating feel like throwing up stop then start 1230
Start walking toward mall stop look back then start 1231
Start walking in town stop then start 1232
Start sewing stop then start 1233
Start doing dishes stop then start 1234
Start jumping stop then start 1235
Start yawning pause start 1236

Start chewing step then start   1237

Start thinking stop then start   1238

THE FOLLOWING CODES ARE IN RELATION TO MEN

Start walking stop then start again   1238

Start eating stop start   1239

Start walking stop then start again   1240

Start eating stop pause start   1241

Start jump stop start   1242

Start eating stop pause start then stop   1243

Start walk start stop then start   1244

Start jump stop start   1245

Start lift stop start   1246

Start eat stop start pause   1247

Start lift stop start pause   1248

Start shift stop start   1249

Start revert stop start   1250

Start digging stop start   1251

Start mince stop start   1252

Start work stop start   1253

Start list stop start   1254

Start listen stop start   1255

Start search stop start   1256

Start jog stop start   1257

Start run stop start   1258

Start yawn stop start   1259

Start eat stop start   1260

Start watch stop start   1261

Start wear clothes stop start   1262

Start wear jeans stop start   1263

Start wear boxer shorts stop start   1264

Start swear stop start   1265

Start sweat stop start   1266

Start vac stop start   1267

Start insist stop start   1268

Start avert start stop   1269

Start jump start stop   1270

Start envy stop start   1271

Start jealous stop pause start   1272

Start malice stop pause start   1273

Start greediness stop pause start 1274

Start cheat stop pause 1275

Start corner stop 1276

Start negotiate stop start 1278

Start comment stop start 1279

Start run stop pause 1280

Start earn stop start 1281

Start new stop pause start 1282

Start imagine pause stop start 1283

Start invigorate pause start 1284

Start negotiate pause start 1285

Start insist pause start 1286

Start attend stop start 1287

Start object stop start 1288

Start renew stop pause start 1289

Start mediate pause stop start 1290

Start adjourn pause stop start 1291

Start adjacent stop 1292

Start renew stop start without pause 1293

Start envy pause stop restart 1294

Start rotate pause start 1295

Start corner pause start 1296

Start negotiate pause stop 1297

Start initiate pause stop start 1298

Start insist pause stop 1299

Start reach pause stop start 1300

Start verify pause start 1301

Start new pause start 1302

Start hurry pause stop start 1303

Start rush stop pause 1304

Start run pause start 1305

Start obey pause start 1306

Start react pause stop 1307

Start insist pause stop start 1308

Start convert stop pause start 1309

Start steer stop start 1310

Start sail stop pause start 1311

Start maneuver pause stop 1312

Start meter pause stop 1313

Start merge pause stop 1314
Stop moving pause start 1315
Stop rotate start 1316
Start aim pause start 1317
Stop maneuver pause start 1318
Stop act stop start 1319
Stop react start 1320
Stop new start stop 1321
Stop react start pause stop start 1322
Start act pause start 1323
Stop means pause stop 1324

Stop react pause start 1325
Start obey pause start 1326
Start annoy pause start 1327
Stop access pause start 1328
Start route pause start 1329
Stop create pause start 1330
Stop react stop start 1331
Stop assess pause start 1332
Stop recess stop start 1333
Stop recall stop start 1334
Stop army start 1335
Stop react start stop 1336
Stop act start stop 1337
Stop run start 1338
Stop dive pause start 1339
Stop view pause start 1340
Stop view stop pause start 1341
Stop run pause stop 1342
Stop access pause stop 1343
Stop evacuate pause start 1344
Stop imitate pause start 1345
Stop invigorate pause start 1346
Stop dice start 1347
Stop maneuver start pause stop 1348
Stop react stop pause start 1349
Stop vacate start 1350

Stop haunt pause start 1351
Stop react pause start 1352
Stop react start 1353
Stop start   1354
Stop   1355
Stop   1356
Stop   1357
Stop   1358
Stop   1359
Stop   1360
Stop   1361
Stop   1362
Stop   1363
Stop   1364
Stop   1365
Stop   1366
Stop   1367
Stop   1368
Stop   1369
Stop   1370
Stop   1371
Stop   1372
Stop   1373
Stop   1374
Stop   1375
Stop   1376
Stop   1377
Stop   1378
Stop   1379
Stop   1380
Stop   1381
Stop   1382
Stop   1383
Stop   1384
Stop   1385
Stop   1386
Stop   1387
Stop   1388
Stop   1389

Stop 1390
Stop 1391
Stop 1392
Stop 1393
Stop 1394
Stop 1395
Stop 1396
Stop 1397
Stop 1398
Stop 1399
Maintain pace start stop 1400
Maintain posture start stop 1401
Maintain composure start stop 1402
Maintain vitality start stop 1403
Maintain energy start stop 1404
Maintain virality start stop 1405
Maintain altitude start stop 1406
Maintain reserve start stop 1407
Maintain posture start pause stop start 1408
Maintain aspect start pause stop start 1409
Maintain optimality start pause stop start 1410
Maintain stamina start pause stop start 1411
Maintain altitude start pause stop start 1412
Maintain pace for a while then stop 1413
Maintain agility for a while then stop 1414
Maintain dedication for a while then stop 1415
Maintain accuracy for a while ten stop 1416
Maintain robustness for a while then stop 1417
Maintain peacefulness for a while then start 1418
Maintain integrity for a while then start 1419
Maintain eloquence for a while then start 1420
Maintain stamina for a while then stop 1421
Maintain robustness for a while then stop 1422
Maintain integrity for a while then stop 1423
Maintain eloquence for a while when stop 1424
While maintaining progress pause then start 1425
While in a rush slow down then start 1426
While in an emergency slow down but start 1427
While in a quiet place speed then stop 1428

While at night slow then stop 1429
While in rush check slow then start. 1430
1431
1462

Other number codes to be added in next volume.

Feel heat 1700
Feel love 1701
Feel hate 1702
Feel lazy 1703
Feel energy 1704
Feel rage 1705
Feel neglected 1706
Feel danger 1707
Feel annoyed 1708
Feel heat on face 1709
Feel hate in head 1710
Feel heat on hands 1711
Feel heat on mouth 1712
Feel heat on fingertips 1713
Feel heat on hands 1714
Feel heat on right hand 1715
Feel heat on left hand 1716
Feel heat on small finger 1717
Feel heat on ring finger 1718
Feel heat on middle finger 1719
Feel heat on index finger 1720
Feel heat on thumb 1721
Feel heat on palm 1722
Feel heat on skin 1723
Feel heat on legs 1724
Feel heat on hands 1725
Feel heat on stomach 1726
Feel heat on lips 1727
Feel heat on left leg 1728
Feel heat on right leg 1729
Feel heat on right hand 1730
Feel heat on left hand 1731
Feel heat on fingertips 1732

Feel heat on cheeks 1733
Feel heat on face cheek left 1734
Feel heat on face cheek right 1735
Feel heat on face check left 1736
Feel heat on inner hand left 1737
Feel heat on hands when on fireplace. 1738
Feel heat when no tire is there 1739
Feel heat on legs when a woman 1740
Feel heat on legs when a woman left leg 1741
Feel heat on legs when a woman right leg 1742
Feel heat on legs when man left leg 1743
Feel heat on legs when a man right leg 1744
Feel heat on tongue when a woman 1745
Feel heat on tongue when a man 1746
Feel heat on private parts for a woman 1747
Feel heat on private parts for a man 1748
Feel heat on elbow if a woman 1749
Feel heat on elbow if a man 1750
Feel heat all body 1751
Feel heat all body if you are a man 1752
Feel heat all body if you are a woman. 1753
Feel heat on back if a woman. 1754
Feel heat on back if you are a man. 1755
Feel the heat when you are walking. 1756
Feel heat when walking in the sun 1757
Feel heat when walking on ice. 7158
Feel heat in the mountains 1759
Feel heat inside the house 1760
Feel heat inside the kitchen 1761
Feel heat inside sitting room 1762
Feel heat inside bedroom 1763
Feel heat inside toilet 1764
Feel heat inside bathroom shower 1765
Feel heat inside toilet at night 1766
Feel heat in the morning 1767
Feel heat in the afternoon 1768
Feel heat in the afternoon 1769
Feel heat in the evening 1770
Feel heat at midnight 1771

Feel the heat in the ocean. 1772

Feel heat in the sand at sea 1773

Feel heat then go into the sea 1774

Feel heat at the pier of the sea 1775

Feel energy 1776

Feel rage 1777

Feel anger 1778

Feel anger at a woman 1779

Feel anger at a man 1780

Feel anger at animal 1781

Feel anger at no one 1782

Feel anger at everyone 1783

Feel anger at yourself 1784

Feel anger at the world 1785

Feel anger at God 1786

Feel anger at no one first then at someone 1787

Feel anger at no one then point at one person. 1788

Feel anger at no one then blame everyone. 1789

Feel anger at the system 1790

Feel anger at work 1791

Feel anger at the manager 1792

Feel anger at no one but while at work 1793

Feel anger at everyone enough to shoot them all. 1794

Feel anger then resort to violence 1795

Feel anger at everyone then blame yourself 1796

Feel anger at everyone then buy a gun 1797

Feel anger at no one then shoot anyone 1798

Feel anger at no one then point at one then apologize without any harm done 1799

Feel anger at one but divert anger at everyone enough at everyone enough to shoot all 1800

Feel anger at leader then attack his supporters 1801

Feel anger at leader then target others not related or involved 1802

Feel anger at leader then target his family 1803

Feel anger at leader then resort to violence of his supporters 1804

Feel anger at leader then raise concerns 1805

Feel anger at leader fail to complain but later decide to kill him 1806

Feel anger at leader but kill his deputy 1804

Feel anger at leader but blame his supporters without pointing at him
1805
Feel anger at war   1806
Feel anger at soldiers killing women and children   1807
Feel anger at all army   1808
Feel anger at all soldiers regardless   1809
Feel anger at doctors regardless   1810
Feel anger at all doctors but enough to kill one or two 1811
Feel anger at a specific doctor but tell someone else to kill them
1812
Feel anger at a specific doctor enough to kill him and buys a gun.
1813
Feel anger at ex.   1814
Feel anger at your x, lover.   1815
Feel rage at your ex.   1816
Feel anger at everyone looking at you   1817
Feel anger at everyone looking at you   1818
Feel anger at everyone you do not like 1819
Feel anger at a priest who is not right   1820
Feel anger at a holy man.   1821
Feel anger at someone then point at all of them enough to shoot all
1822
Feel rage at one but keep quiet planning how to revenge and punish
1823
Feel anger at one then you get a gun and go after that person. 1824
Feelings at all but pick just one who is to tell   1825
Feel anger at all then ask someone else to just point at one.   1826
Feel rage at all then isolate one and go after him   1827
Feel rage at all but choose to ignore all 1828
Feelings at all but blame no one 1833 feel anger at all but drop the
anger   1829
Feel anger at some but blame all   1830
Feel anger at none but act to kill all   1831
Feel anger at all but ask them to change or else.   1832
Feel anger at all but ask all to change then target just one   1833
Feel anger at public place shout and scream then kick this but calm
soon after.   1834
Feel rage in public place then threaten to kill but walk away.   1835
Feel rage at someone but pick no one then shoot a stranger.   1836

Feel anger at someone but keep it a secret befriend that person
1837

Feel anger at someone then befriend them then drop all the rage
after.   1838

Feel anger at one then pick on innocent person   1839

Feel anger at one then ask a stranger to kill that person.   1840

Feel anger at one then go after that one until he or she is dead.
1841

Feel rage then attack a different but related person.   1842

Feel rage then attack that person but calm no guilt deserved to die.
1843

Feel rage at one then kill all his children first and leave him alive.
1844

Feel rage at one then kill all his kids including him or her.   1845

Feel rage at one point then kill his children him or her cats and dogs
too.   1846

Feel rage then kill all his children, him or her pets and claim he
deserved to die.   1847

Feel rage with others but curse at the word   1848

Feel rage with leaders but secretly plan to ambush them   1849

Feel rage with the leaders but confronts them just to warn them.
1850

Feel rage but do nothing   1851

Feel rage and resort to violence on others not involved   1852

Feel rage and attack source of rage and not others unrelated.   1853

Feel rage but decide to research first before taking action   1854

Feel rage at everyone but research first before planning all   1855

Feel anger at all then screen all one by one to find who is to blame
1856

Feel rage at oneself but blame others   1857

Feel rage at oneself and blames oneself.   1858

Feel rage with everyone but ignore all on sight on seeing them.
1859

Feel rage and forgiveness.   1860

Feel rage on everyone but select the right wrong doer and go after
him until he or she is dead.   1861

Feel rage on others but keep it a distance.   1862

Feel rage and attack all of them   1863

Feel rage and attack all country.   1864

Feel rage and forgive the culprits. 1865

Feel rage attacks but forgive. 1866

Feel rage promise to kill in public. 1867

Feel rage and promise to kill in public. 1868

Feel rage and promise to deal with them now or forever. 1868

Feel rage and promise justice in the end. 1869

Feel rage and act to fulfill promise without failure 1870

Feel rage and report to authorities then act to get justice. 1879

Feel rage 1880

Feel rage 1881

Feel rage 1882

Feel rage 1883

Feel rage 1884

Feel rage 1885

Feel rage 1886

Feel rage 1887

Feel rage 1888

Feel rage 1889

Feel rage 1890

Feel rage 1891

Feel rage 1892

Feel rage 1893

Feel love to a woman. 1946

Feel love to others 1948

Feel love to everyone 1949

Feel love to wrongdoers 1950

Feel love to others 1951

Feel strong feelings towards others. 1952

Feel strong love for other races. 1953

Feel strong love to own race 1954

Feel love to all women regardless of race and religion. 1955

Mediate start pause stop	2001
Mediate act pause stop	2002
Mediate react pause stop	2003
Mediate stop pause stop	2004
Mediate react stop	2005
Mediate assess stop start	2006
Mediate take stop start	2007
Mediate talk stop start	2008
Mediate ask stop start	2009
Mediate assess pause	2010
Mediate react pause	2011
Mediate act pause	2012
Mediate assess pause	2013
Mediate ask pause	2014
Mediate jolt pause	2015
Mediate react pause	2016
Mediate teach pause	2017
Mediate open pause	2018
Mediate react pause	2019
Mediate ask pause	2020
Mediate rotate pause	2021
Mediate note pause	2022
Mediate alter pause	2023
Mediate react pause	2024
Mediate act pause	2025
Mediate answer pause	2026
Mediate ask pause	2027
Mediate rotate pause	2028
Mediate annotate pause	2029
Mediate ask pause	2030

More codes to be added in the next book.

ABOUT DAVID GOMADZA

I am the First Global President Of The World
Visit
www.twofuture.world
info@twofuture.world
00447719210295